Dedicated to my children:
Elizabeth Grace Yana-April 1986
Adrienne, Joy and Caleb
And my grandchildren:
Quinten, Adeline, Runa,
Mailee and Earthyn

Created for:

Mabel Oppong and her school kids;

Kumasi, Ghana Africa

ISBN-13: 978-1984993960
ISBN-10: 1984993968

To be used in conjunction with "Noah" (ISBN-13: 978-1981458622)

www.truthdiscovered.net

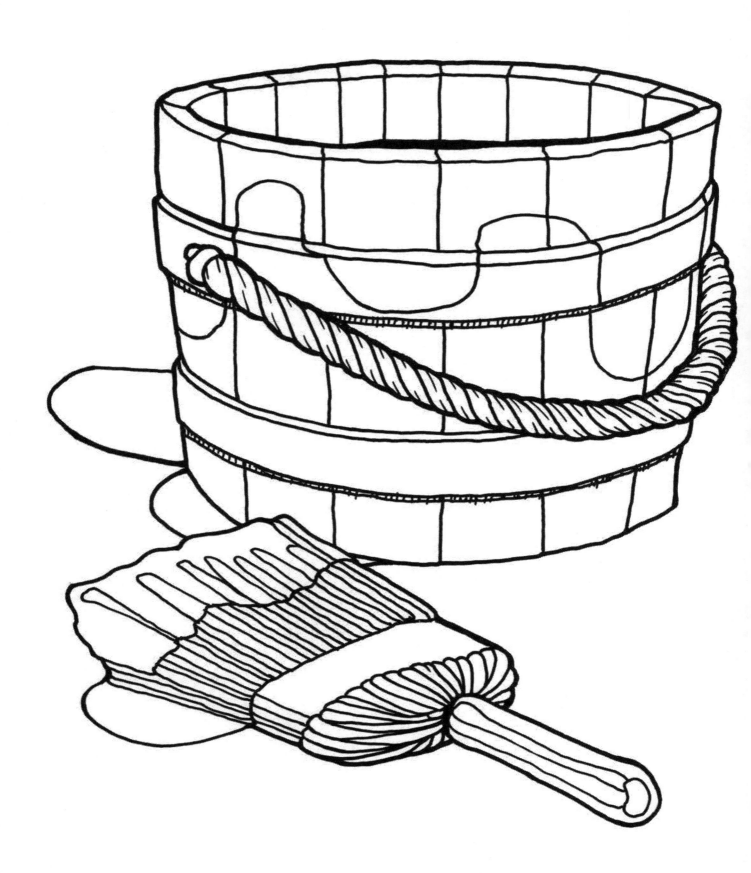

Color match each country to its pre-flood position on the globe.

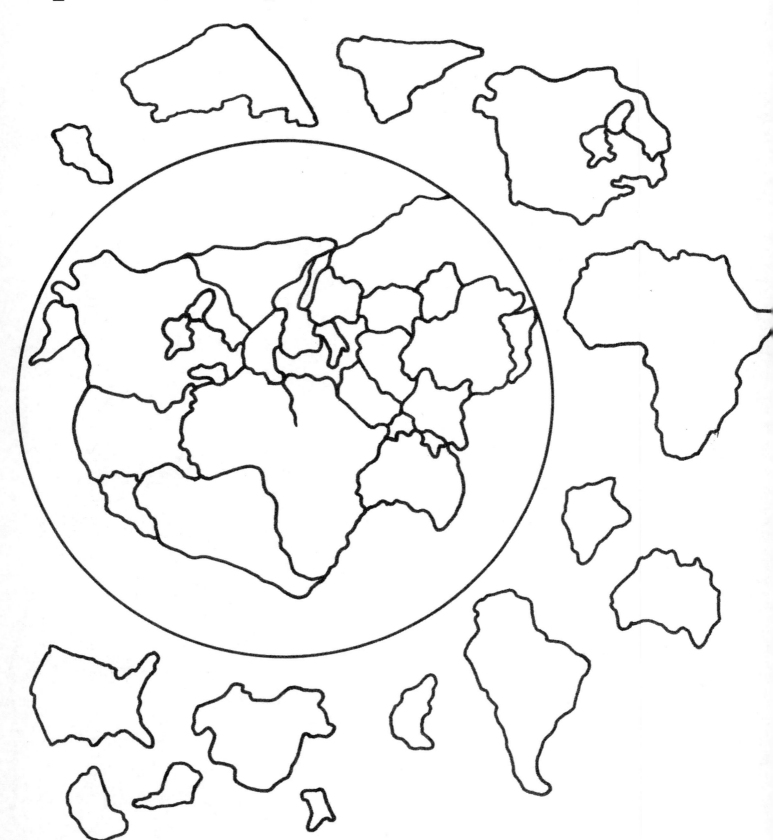

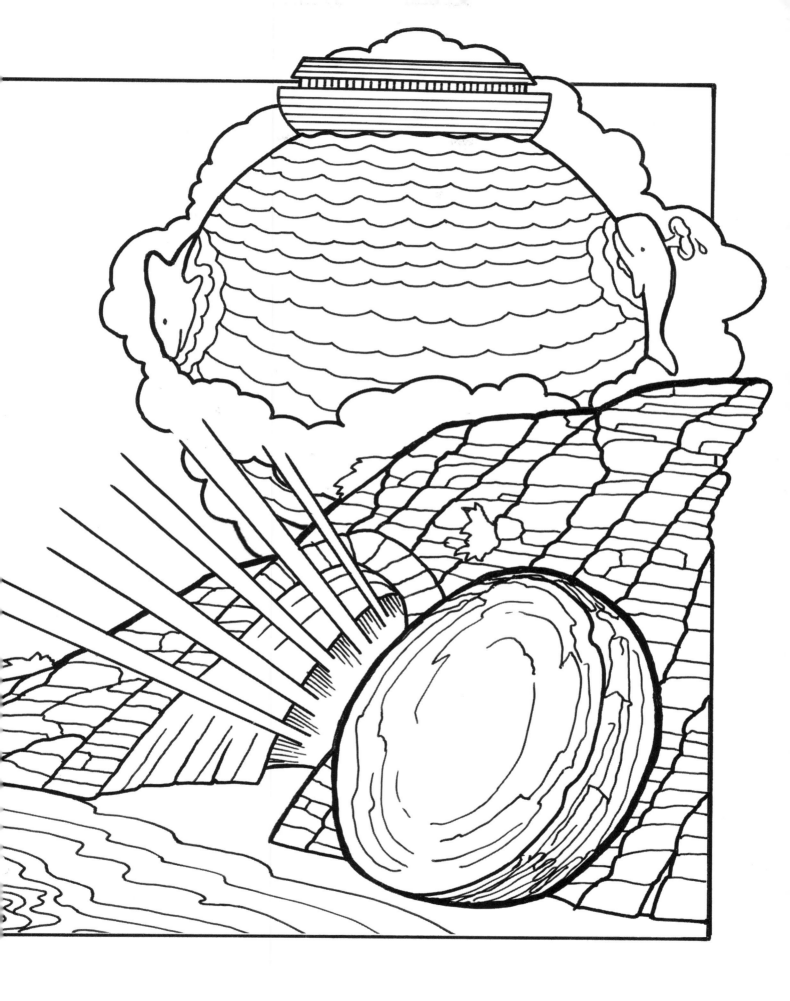